DOGS
of ALL SIZES

DOGS
of ALL SIZES

by NINA LEEN

AMPHOTO
American Photographic Book Publishing Co., Inc.
Garden City, N.Y. 11530

Published in Garden City, New York by American Photographic
Book Publishing Company, Inc.
Pictures previously taken for *Life* Magazine
reprinted here with the permission of Time, Inc.
Library of Congress Catalog Card No. 74-76682

ISBN: 0-8174-0567-4

Manufactured in the United States of America

Layout Design by Nina Leen

Thanks to Some People...

Whenever I needed information or advice,
Mr. and Mrs. Hendrik Van Rensselaer and
Thomas Pescod, D.V.M., patiently answered all my
questions. Patricia Maye, Managing Editor of Amphoto,
who encouraged me to do this book in the first place,
often renewed my shaky self-confidence with her
cheerful "Keep going, you're doing fine!"
And, as usual, everybody in the Time-Life lab
deserves a big *Thank You* for their help.

N. L.

CONTENTS

Introduction 7

Small Dogs 11

Poodles 34

Medium Dogs 40

Large Dogs 56

Exercise 74

Grooming 90

Puppies 101

SKYE TERRIER

INTRODUCTION

This is not meant to be a guide book to dog breeding. I am not competent to give advice on medical care or training and I don't pretend to be an authority on dog behavior. But, in my work, I met a good number of different breeds, read a great deal about them, observed them, and lived with dogs of my own for many years. I don't think that "all dogs like me"—some do, others couldn't care less about me, but I never expect unconditional affection. I care about *them* and to me that is enough reason for my doing this book.

Usually, every pedigreed dog is classified by category: the Sporting Dogs, the Non-Sporting Dogs, the Working Dogs, the Hounds, the Terriers, the Toy Dogs. But people who buy a pet dog are not generally concerned as to whether he belongs to the Sporting Dogs, the Working Dogs, or any other group. Most often the main consideration is the size. To simplify matters, I grouped the breeds into three categories—Small, Medium, and Large.

"Small" is a dog you can carry unobserved within a roomy bag or a folded sweater into places with inhospitable signs reading "No Dogs." Small is a dog to whom your two-room apartment seems as big as a ball field. He can be trained to use a newspaper-lined box in the bathroom corner when outdoors a blizzard or gale-force wind might sweep him away. In trains and taxicabs, you can hold him on your lap without the least discomfort. If he's too big for that he belongs in the next category—Medium.

"Medium" is probably what your dog and your neighbors' dogs are. Some of the most popular breeds belong in this category. Classically, they grow up with the children and follow them to a nearby school in the country. They are so popular that their images are used to promote products that are definitely *not* for dog consumption. For many years, the Fox Terrier was to be seen intently listening to "his master's voice" on gramophone records. Today, two Scotties pose proudly on a label, selling Scotch. Medium-sized breeds are not too large to share small quarters with their owners but they are large enough to effectively scare off an intruder. If this sounds like a plug for the "Mediums," it is not intended to be. No one should tell you what breed or type of dog to choose, because it often happens that people find themselves the delighted owners of a dog they never thought of buying in the first place.

"Large" is a category that most people have made their minds up about. The belief is that they need a *special way of life*. This is a misconception. "Large dogs belong in the country" is a statement that sounded right years ago. People living in the country had gardens, fields, or woods surrounding their houses. The dog could roam about with no fences, no traffic, no dognappers, no leash laws. Country dogs lived until they died from natural causes. Suburbs looked like suburbs. Families had houses that their parents had owned before them and it was natural to have a big dog. Rarely did a family sell the big house and move away. Today, they do. They change jobs and relocate in the city or they rent apartments in the new skyscrapers that the suburbs are full of. And, what happens to the large dog who has lived half of his life with them in the country? Do they trade him in for a smaller model? Some are abandoned (yes, pure-breds too) in the slim and overly optimistic hope that they will find another good home on their own. They seldom do. So don't fall prey to the false notion that a large dog is only a country dog.

When people buy a dog it is for life—for the dog's life. Where the dog lives out that life is up to his master. It seems to me that as long as they are together, any life is alright with the dog.

A YORKSHIRE TERRIER PUPPY

SMALL DOGS

If the appearance of small dogs coincided with the invention of efficiency apartments, compact cars, or rising food prices, it could be judged a natural phenomenon. But for thousands of years, tiny toy dogs have belonged to and been loved by some of the most important people in history. In summer the Romans travelled to Pompeii with their tiny companions. Through the centuries, in many priceless paintings, the little dog has occupied a prominent place in the foreground. It is obvious that nothing should obscure the noble pet—not even his royal master. Occasionally, the tiny dogs are represented displaying character traits inherited from their much larger ancestors. They are seen taking on other dogs many times their size, defending their masters, and always seeming oblivious to their own reduced scale.

The appealing fact that a dog, whose love and loyalty is so comforting, and who is loved in return, can easily be toted around was probably the reason for breeding the Toys. Undoubtedly, people in ancient times had the same need for affection as people today. If you take your small dog "everywhere you go" as the Romans did, please, do *carry* him in crowded places. Sometimes in busy department stores, I see delicate little dogs trying to dodge menacing, giant feet and each time I feel as if I am watching a terrifying horror movie. "Will *they* crush him or will *he* survive?"

But what if the Giant trips over the Lilliputian and suffers a bad fall? Let's not even think of that!

AFFENPINCHER

The black terrier, with dark sparkling eyes and a shaggy, bewhiskered face, can look frightening to an aggressor. He usually has a quiet dignity, but when faced with danger, this tiny "monkey terrier" becomes a ball of fire and will courageously confront an enemy much larger than himself. He can be traced back to 17th century Germany where his ancestors did rat-catching. Regardless of his unglamorous past, strange looks, and fiery temper, the Affenpincher became a lady's favorite. Devoted and smart, he knows how to win friends.

LONG COAT CHIHUAHUA

The long-haired variety of the tiny Chihuahua is seldom seen on city streets. With soft and silky hair, the two and one-half pound dog seems born to thrive among velvet pillows and luxurious carpets. But in reality, smooth or long-haired, he is the same intelligent, active little dog.

LHASA APSO

For over 800 years the small, hairy terriers, originally from the sacred city of Lhasa beyond the Himalayas, served as guard dogs in the monasteries and homes of Tibet. Before they became popular worldwide, the Lhasa Apsos belonged exclusively to the household of the Dali Lama and were never for sale but were presented only as gifts.

AUSTRALIAN TERRIER

The early settlers of Australia brought the ancestors of today's breed along with them from England to kill rodents. The little dog with a lot of personality has become increasingly popular since. He need not kill rodents anymore to be appreciated and loved.

BRUSSELS GRIFFON
Named after the mythical Gryphon—a monstrous beast, part lion and part eagle, who guarded Asian goldmines and treasures —today's Griffon is alert, affectionate, and easy to live with. He has the color of a lion and the inquisitive look of the eagle.

POMERANIAN
One of the smallest dogs, the lively Pomeranian has an impressive line-up of much larger relatives: Alaskan Malamute, Chow Chow, Spitz, and Norwegian Elkhound. Pom was a great favorite of England's Queen Victoria and still has his fans all over the world.

YORKSHIRE TERRIER

YORKSHIRE TERRIER

He may look like a toy but this dog is all terrier. Many years ago, the miners in Yorkshire, England needed a stout-hearted little dog to hunt underground and bred the first Yorkshires to meet their need. In recent years, the little Yorky has become extremely fashionable, sometimes serving its master solely as a status symbol. But many owners have discovered to their delight that beyond being beautiful, the Yorkshire has many varied and delightful characteristics. Like a true terrier, he is a good swimmer and can keep his head above water until a high wave hits him. Even that may damage his hairdo but not his spirit.

Yorkies make friends where they find them. This young puppy found a big, white, soft rabbit at a neighbor's barn. He visits him daily to sit, or sleep, at his side.

The little terrier can even be trained to hunt. He is too small to retrieve a large bird but he can learn to point and the high grass does not impede him.

All manner of tricks can the Yorky learn.
For a dog candy, he will dance around
until his mistress rewards him.

PUG

In the 17th century, the Pug arrived in Europe aboard the ships of the Dutch East India Company. His original home was probably China but he transplanted well and very soon after his landing he became *the* dog in the palaces of most European countries. From time to time, the long-haired toy breeds make people forget the Pug but there is no danger of the breed vanishing. He invariably comes back—as popular as ever.

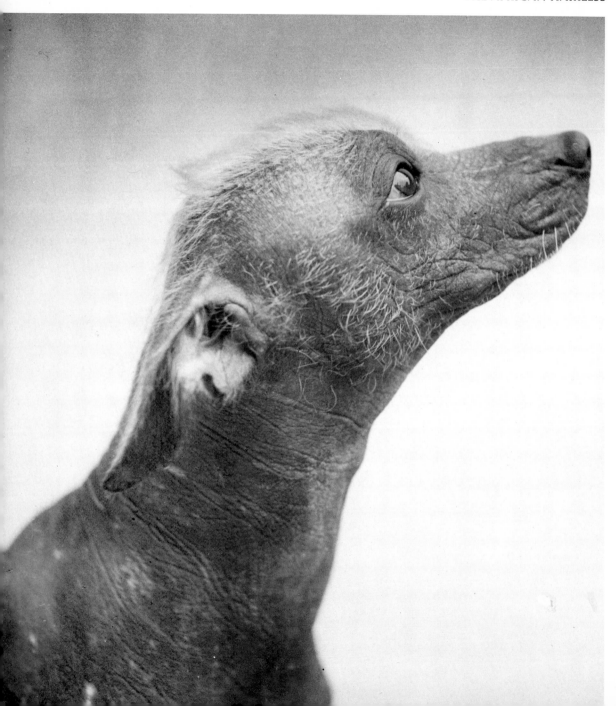

These hairless dogs come from Central Africa where their ancestors hunted elephants with their masters. Their gray skin looks very much like the skin of the elephant, but the resemblance stops there. They are soft and warm. Walking barometers, their color changes with the weather—light gray when the weather is fair, dark and dull when it gets bad. The African Hairless is also known as the Small African Greyhound or the Nubian Dog.

This African Hairless may look like a
Dachshund but he can do what a Dachshund
never can do—he can put *up* his ears if he
wants to.

They have no hair.
and less teeth than other dogs,
but the appetite
is the same.

MINIATURE DACHSHUND
High on the popularity scale, the little Dachshund is irresistible. His antics make people laugh—it is hard to keep a straight face when he jumps around the room or even just looks at you. He greets strangers with a challenging bark but soon decides that his master's friends are his friends and suddenly rolls over.

MALTESE

For 3000 years, the little snow-white dog from Malta in the Mediterranean has been a favorite of royalty. His island home was famous for its riches and "the ancient dog of Malta" long lived there in rare luxury. Today he makes a fine and friendly pet. Small under all that hair, four Maltese can travel in one middle-sized basket carrier.

CHIHUAHUA

The smallest dogs anywhere in the world were discovered about 125 years ago in the Mexican state of Chihuahua. It proved a lucky find. The tiny dogs, weighing an average of two to three pounds, soon became a popular sensation. Today, the Chihuahua's popularity is still on the rise.

Unlike many other small breeds, the Chihuahua is not just a lady's pet.
Many men like his personality. He is exceptionally intelligent, lively,
and a good deal of dog—despite his tiny size.

MINIATURE SCHNAUZER

The handsome miniature breed is a close relative to the larger-scale Standard Schnauzer. Native to Germany, this dog has but one love in his life—his master. A sociable fellow, he will always prefer to be in the company of people than to romp with other dogs.

NORWICH TERRIER

First bred in Norwich, England around
1880, the litle rough-coated dog proves
to be a faithful house pet and courageous
outdoor hunter. The mother Norwich
teaches her pups all they'll need to know
to be good terriers.

POODLES

The Poodle has a unique position in the dog world. The same dog, identical in every part, comes in three sizes—Standard, Miniature, and Toy. He can be black, white, gray, silver, blue, brown, café-au-lait, apricot or cream. The browns, café-au-laits, and apricots may have liver-colored noses, but all other Poodle noses are black. There is a selection of clips that the Poodle owner may choose from: the Puppy Clip—with or without moustache; the English Saddle Clip; the Continental Clip; the Royal Dutch Clip; and the Utility Clip.

Whole industries cater to the Poodle clientele. Beauty parlors specializing in poodle grooming, accessories with poodles engraved, unusual carriers and velvet-lined beds for the Toy, could drive other dog owners to using tranquilizers. With unbelievable imagination, the dog-fashion designers create exclusive originals for Poodles like hand-embroidered sweaters, pajamas, raincoats, and jewelry. The Poodle accepts all the luxury with good-natured dignity seemingly to please his owner. He is very intelligent.

Things were not always so posh. The Poodle's life was different only a few centuries ago. He was a water dog, renowned wild duck retriever, and excellent swimmer. His clip was not invented originally to give him a startling appearance—it was simply a practical way to protect his joints and the upper part of his body in icy water. In France, his name is *Caniche* from *canard*—duck—a continuing reminder of his rough and rugged past.

The ancestry of the Poodle is a mystery yet to be solved. France claims him as her own but so do Germany, England, Italy, Spain, Portugal, and Russia. Someone must be right.

The Miniature Poodle is smaller than the Standard—larger than the Toy. He seems always to be fully aware of the importance of his appearance. Even when resting, he is not going to spoil his hairdo.

The Toy Poodle is the smallest member of the Poodle family. Many centuries ago, Toys became favorites of German, Spanish, and French society and are today still as popular as ever.

Poodles present many faces to the world. Basically always the same dog, they can look like entirely different breeds. The large Standard sometimes wears a jewelled barrette to hold back his hair.

This Toy with a Royal Dutch Clip is wearing a genuine gold-and-pearl chain around his neck. Toy owners are an exclusive club of people, dedicated to this little dog and willing to spend time and money on this four-footed member of the family.

The Standard Poodle is often seen in the simple and handsome Utility Clip.

Small and large pupils, equally intelligent, learn good behavior at an obedience class for poodles only. Except for one rebel, the class listens attentively and follows commands. Poodles quickly learn to master various tricks and frequently become circus and stage attractions.

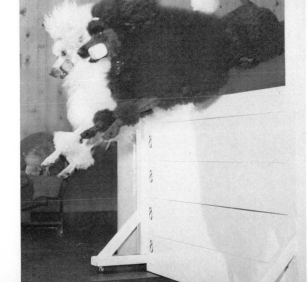

◄ Two students, a Toy and a Standard, eagerly await their turn.

MEDIUM DOGS

Perhaps the best known members of the "Mediums" are the Cocker and Beagle. Well adapted to city or country life, loyal and affectionate, they are the established American family dogs. Some of the less known breeds, like the Basenji, Bedlington, Puli, and Bull Terrier, are still conversation pieces on city streets but are rapidly gaining in popularity.

The barkless Basenji is most appreciated by apartment house neighbors. He can't bark but he *can* yodel. As a watchdog, his yodel wouldn't scare a soul, but his rumbling, deep growl and bared teeth will impress a stranger.

The Puli is a born supervisor. As a member of the family, he takes care of everyone—especially the children—and even considers the baby to be his personal responsibility. Since he is a shepherd dog, herding is in his blood and guarding a flock of sheep or his human family is of equal importance to him.

Today's Bull Terrier is not a vicious dog. He is devoted and fearless. His past glorious fighting career will come back to him if he sees his master threatened or attacked.

The Bedlington has a useful characteristic: his coat does not shed. Everyone knows what a plus that can be in keeping a nice, neat apartment hairless.

The dogs in this category often prove to be "the happy medium" in making the choice between a large dog or a small one. Each has characteristics appreciated in today's life: These may be the reasons why they have become so welcome.

MINIATURE POODLE ►
Louis XVI of France introduced the Poodle to his court and since that time no other dog can look so magnificent as His Majesty the Poodle.

SKYE TERRIER

The terrier with the long, beautiful, blanket-like coat covering his body from head to tail was first bred on the Isle of Skye in the Hebrides. His devotion is legendary—a memorial in Edinburgh commemorates one Skye who kept a ten-year vigil at the grave of his master.

WHIPPET

The dog, which seems to have
emerged from a medieval tapestry,
is known for his speed and grace.
In England he is used as a racing dog
and over a short distance can run
at a speed of 45 miles an hour.
The Whippet likes the country life
but will be happy in a city home if
he can be close to his master.

FRENCH BULLDOG

A compact dog with bat ears and a naturally short tail, the French Bulldog was bred especially to serve as a gentle companion in Parisian homes.

BASSET HOUND

The unusual-looking Basset is bred in the United States. His Bloodhound head seems too big for the Dachshund body and his loose coat looks several sizes too large. But behind this strange façade is a smart and engaging personality.

DANDY DINMONT
The terrier from Scotland is the clown of the dog world. He can always invent some funny trick to amuse his human audience. The lovable breed was named after a character in a Walter Scott novel.

PULI
Over 1,000 years ago, the Puli came to Hungary with Asiatic invaders.
Hairy and shaggy, he looks like a smaller, ragged version of the English
Sheepdog. An excellent herder, the Puli really likes his work.

Devoted to herding sheep, the Puli does not take his duty lightly. No sheep in his herd can run away unnoticed. With expert skill, the Puli leaps on the runaway and rides it gently back to the herd.

All the sheep are back, but the Puli
is always on guard.

BEDLINGTON TERRIER

The Bedlington may look like a lamb, but behind his deceiving appearance is a lively, courageous terrier. The breed comes from Great Britain where a mason in Bedlington gave his favorite dogs the city's name.

The Puli knows the difference. This "lamb" is his playmate, a Bedlington.

BASENJI

The ancestry of the barkless dog of Africa can be traced back to Egypt in the 4th century B.C. Still popular on his native continent, today the Basenji goes off to the hunt with a bell on his neck. An ideal pet in the city, the Basenji is devoted and quiet. His coat is glossy and odorless and he cleans himself like a cat.

BEAGLE

For over 1500 years, the Beagle has been bred and loved in England. A tiny version of the breed was produced for Queen Elizabeth I, so small that they were called "pocket beagles" and indeed they could be carried in a pocket. When the standard beagle came to America, he quickly won hearts all over the country. A favorite on the farm and a loved pet in the city, his patience with small children is astounding and he proves to be gentle, good-natured, and loving toward every member of the family.

BULL TERRIER

In the 19th century in Great Britain, Bull Terriers were professional fighters. They were bred to fight and to like it. Today, that is all past history—pit fights are against the law in England and the Bull Terrier now has a different goal in life. He is a watchful, dependable, strong and very courageous pet.

COCKER SPANIEL

The American Cocker is always described as "the dog with a good disposition." He is gentle with children and likes everyone. A very adaptable companion, he can adjust to many different ways of life. One Cocker, who belonged to a sea captain, travelled around the oceans for 13 years; another often parachuted to earth with his master.

FOX TERRIER

Highly intelligent, the Fox Terrier learns tricks quickly and often becomes a boy's best friend.

Fox hunting in England gave this terrier its name. The breed is equally popular on both sides of the Atlantic. First, it was the smooth-haired variety that won everyone's admiration. Then came the wire-haired, whose American popularity was boosted by the appearance of Asta in the "Thin Man" movies.

WIRE-HAIRED FOX TERRIER
Few dogs can look so exquisite as a well-groomed Wire.

LARGE DOGS

The physical and personality characteristics of large dogs are as different as the dogs themselves. Most belong to people who like a dog best when there is at least 50 pounds of him and will do everything in their power to keep their large-sized pets healthy and happy.

The good-natured giants in this category seem to recognize their own size and its possible embarrassing consequences. In close quarters, they move with care and grace around furniture, amazingly keeping their tails from sweeping the dishes off the coffee table, and avoiding even the slightest destruction.

One of the largest breeds, the Great Dane, is a home-loving dog. He wants only to be with his owner and does not care to roam the streets or countryside by himself. Other large dogs share this attachment to the human way of life. Mountains of hair, like the Bobtail and Chow Chow, ride in tiny cars, travel on airplanes, and take the sophisticated lifestyle of a 20th century dog for granted.

The days of wild boar hunting, fighting in wars alongside noble knights, and whatever else the big dogs did are over. Now their masters live differently and so do the dogs. Some of them, having a generous yard or field to run in, will wait patiently outside the door for someone to come out and play with them. In the city, the owners go out of their way to exercise them, while in the country it is not unusual to see a large dog drowsing all day on the porch. "If that's what he wants!" is the usual resigned comment of the master. There is no rule for *all* dogs —each is an individual.

AFGHAN HOUND ►

When Noah launched his ark, two Afghans were the dogs aboard—so the story goes. Carvings in the ancient tombs found in the valley of the Nile show the Afghan, but the Western world did not believe that this curious looking dog was anything more than an artist's invention. The Afghan proved real when he was discovered living in the hills of Afghanistan where rock carvings dated around 2200 B.C. show him hunting. This beautiful dog continued to inspire artists into our own time. The modern master Picasso often depicted his Afghan, Kaboul, in his paintings. Afghan Hounds come in different colors--cream, fawn, and black seem to be the most popular.

SALUKI

Known to have lived in the Near East over 5000 years ago, the Saluki is probably the oldest pure breed in existence today. His original home may have been the long-vanished town of Saluk in Arabia. Because of his speed and grace, the beautiful Saluki holds a unique position with his Arab masters—he is allowed to share the tent at night and is often the most highly prized possession of a desert sheik. Having "the beauty of the thoroughbred horse" is the way the American Kennel Club describes the Saluki.

OTTERHOUND

With his webbed feet, the Otterhound is a
skillful swimmer. His dense coat keeps him
comfortable in the chilly river when he
hunts otters at night.

IBIZAN HOUND

During the Ninth Century, the Ibizan Hound came from Egypt to the Balearic Island of Ibiza in the Mediterranean. The Ibizan is an intelligent and active dog. He has acute senses of smell and hearing, is a good hunter, and can find his way even in thick underbrush by night.

BOXER

The rugged-looking Boxer comes from Germany where the breed first appeared about a hundred years ago. The Great Dane and the Bulldog are among his ancestors—there is a definite resemblance to both these breeds. Appearing in many shades of brown with white markings (not more than one third of the body should be white according to breed standards), the Boxer is a perfect family dog. Cool to strangers, he saves all his affection for the people to whom he belongs.

BULLDOG ►

Fifty five pounds is the correct weight for a champion Bulldog. In past centuries these dogs were bred for ferocious fights with bulls in special "sports" arenas. Today's Bulldog has an appealing ugliness. There is nothing vicious in his character—he is courageous but hard to provoke. It is hard to find a more peace-loving dog than the fierce looking Bulldog.

BLOODHOUND

In the Eighth Century, the monks of the Saint Hubert Monastery in Belgium developed a breed that they named the "Dog of Saint Hubert." Centuries later, when these dogs came to live in monasteries in Britain, the breed was kept pure and renamed "blooded hound." This is but one version of why this dog is today called the "Bloodhound." His ability to track down people—whether lost or fugitive—makes him an important factor in police work. Looking determined and grim, he may appear aggressive—but his quarry has nothing to be afraid of. The Bloodhound is gentle and affectionate, happy to see even the most unfriendly fugitive he has just tracked down.

WEIMARANER

Breeding of the original Weimaraners was controlled by strict rules. Only a small group in Weimar, Germany even knew that this dog existed. Owners had to belong to an exclusive club and even they could not own more than three or four dogs. Outsiders were shunned. No one could buy a Weimaraner if three club members voted against it. By agreement, inferior puppies were destroyed to keep a top standard. The gray dogs with amber eyes eventually came to America. Breeding is still controlled but the breed is becoming more and more popular.

DALMATIAN

Coach dog, fire engine mascot, or playful family companion, the Dalmatian makes friends wherever he goes. He is easy to train and eager to please.

GREAT DANE

Despite the name, the breed did not originate in Denmark. The Great Dane was bred in Germany to hunt, guard castles, and accompany his noble master. The Dane is called "king among dogs" and no other dog can dispute his title.

GERMAN SHEPHERD

Some experts believe that the German Shepherd's ancestry goes back to the Bronze Age dog of 6000-7000 B.C. Others think that he lived and worked since ancient times in Germany. Whatever his origins, this dog has produced more heroes around the world than any other breed. The Shepherd served with dependable intelligence and courage during both World Wars, assists police in many countries, and is known to have given his life to fulfill an assignment. The picture of Rin Tin Tin, the movie idol, looking over the landscape from a high rock, is better known than paintings of history's great generals surveying the battlefild from similar vantage points.

CHOW CHOW ►

The "black-tongued dog" is one of the many names for the furry Chinese dog with the blue-black tongue. About 200 years ago, trading ships from Asia brought these dogs to England along with other assorted cargo. To simplify things, the traders declared their imports in pidgin English as "Chow chow." Ever since, the breed has kept its amusing name. The Chow descends from an ancient breed and appears in 2000-year-old Chinese carvings. He is dignified, proud, and independent. It is sad to report that in some Asiatic countries this breed is raised to be served as a delicacy.

OLD ENGLISH SHEEPDOG

His popular name is "Bobtail."
When the Sheepdog herded
sheep in his native England,
his tail had to be bobbed—the
usual requirement for a
working dog. The giant mop
has a playful, charming
personality which he is able
to project through pounds of
shaggy hair. Wherever he
appears, all eyes follow him.
His rolling bearlike gait, free
driving trot, and elastic gallop
are all sure attention getters.

GERMAN SHORT-HAIRED POINTER

A favorite with American
sportsmen, the German
Short-Haired Pointer is a
dependable hunting
companion and a good friend
to have around the house.

SCOTTISH DEERHOUND
"The Royal Dog of Scotland" is a fitting name for the dignified Scot. In past centuries in his native land, no one beneath the rank of earl could own the Deerhound. Today, he is a wonderful companion for anyone living in the country.

IRISH WOLFHOUND
Proud giants of dogdom, the Irish Wolfhounds are the largest breed in the world. They are known to have been kept by the Celts as early as 273 B.C. and in 391 A.D., "Rome viewed them with wonder" when seven of these dogs fought in the imperial circus. The Wolfhound's history through the ages is filled with heroic deeds, but few people know how gentle and devoted these powerful dogs can be.

73

EXERCISE

"Dogs need exercise!" That statement sounds so definitive and final that many people who are considering giving a dog a good home become frightened and abandon the whole idea. They defend their decision against taking in a pet by saying that they can't afford to lose time, sleep, health, and money, even for the most lovable companion.

Such sacrifices are not necessary. If you don't live in a lighthouse surrounded by the ocean—even if you do, running up and down the stairs would be quite an exercise for a dog—you probably have a street, park, or some other available firm ground when you could take a dog for a fifteen-minute walk once or twice every 24 hours. The routine need not affect your work or social life, as it is up to you to decide when you can best spare the time. Some people would never take a healthy daily walk were it not for the dogs in their lives. Even in winter, your health will not suffer if you bundle up according to the weather. Anyway, you can get a cold on the way to work or to the grocery store.

Some exercise can be gotten at home. A simply constructed hurdle, located in a place where your dog can't walk around it, is a useful contraption. With a little encouragement and a dog cookie as a reward, he will jump over the barricade repeatedly. A tug of war, whether indoors or out, is even better for your dog than a walk.

If your dog is trained to come to you when you call (as all good dogs should be), you can have an energetic game of ball with him in a dead-end street or in an empty lot away from traffic.

When you are ready for a dog, don't let the word "exercise" scare you—it is not as bad as it sounds. I have done, with my own dog, everything described here.

The Yorkshire retrieves his dumbbell over a hurdle.

When the weather is bad, nobody wants to take a walk—not even the hardy Dandy Dinmont.

Most dogs know what's good for them. Catching a ball 50 to 60 times is a healthy exercise. If he brings the ball back, all you have to do is throw it again. After a long play session, you may decide that he is exhausted. Usually, you are wrong.

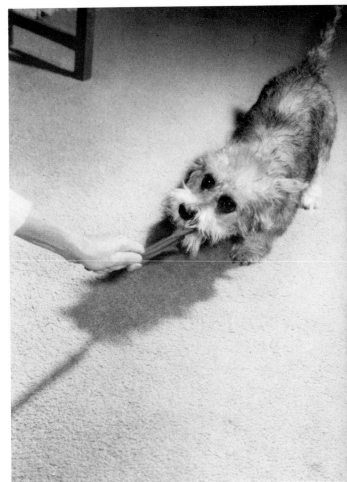

After a short recess, he is back at your side looking sad and rejected. If you don't want to play ball anymore, but can't stand the look in his eyes, there are other ways to make him happy.

Tug-of-war is a good workout for the dog's muscles. It makes both you and him tired but, in most cases, you will win. Not so with a large dog! Be careful and hold on to something heavy—if you don't want to land at his feet.

A West Highland White Terrier is out for a walk. The daily routine for most city dogs is "once around the block." If it is not a brisk walk around several blocks, it won't do any good. If you go windowshopping or stop to chat with friends, the walk may be fun for you but not sufficient exercise for your dog. You must keep walking.

If you take your Irish Setter along to a business appointment, be sure to allow time for his walk to the curb. Otherwise, you may be quite late for your meeting.

On a quiet street with little or no traffic, a child can take the dog out for a run. But no dog should be allowed to run around without a leash. Even on the leash, a lively dog, such as the perky Fox Terrier, in pursuit of adventure, may get himself and the child into trouble.

Far from his native Sahara, a large, fenced-in backyard can offer sufficient space for the slender Saluki to jump, chase balls, gallop around, and have exercise next best to a run in the desert.

The German Short-Haired Pointer makes good his escape through the
open gate. He is in a hurry to play in a small field behind the house.

On a little country road, four Maltese dogs
take a brisk walk on a leash.

Running along behind his master's car at 10 miles per hour, this active Doberman gets his daily exercise.

The Scottish Deerhound is fortunate to live in the country where he can follow his mistress on her daily rides and has ample ground to roam.

One of the largest dogs, the Deerhound likes long walks. Always knowing his way around, he seldom wanders too far from home.

When it is time to go back, the Deerhound turns resolutely toward
familiar landmarks.

On the way home, he jumps a fence with speed and grace—a tribute to his Greyhound blood.

At home, the Deerhound's best friend is a little Schipperke, a tailless black dog from Belgium. Long kept to guard barges in Belgian waters, the Schipperke's name is Flemish for "little captain."

GROOMING

Any dog you live with has to be groomed—by you. If your dog needs special attention, a professional groomer will provide it at the necessary intervals. What you must do from day to day is keep his coat in good shape.

Regardless of his size, your dog has more ways to collect dust than wall-to-wall carpeting. A small dog, looking for his toy, can get into completely inaccessible places where even a broom or vacuum only gets every six months. Running around outdoors in good weather, the dog comes back decorated with little tokens of nature—clumps of earth in his hair, sand between his toes, and burrs, thorns, and dry leaves embedded in his coat. In bad weather, snow, mud, and many other messy things come into the house with him. He will look terrible and later he will deposit part of the unsightly collection on your floors and rugs unless you catch up with him first. You must inspect your dog when he comes in, remove the burrs, clean his paws, dry him if it is wet outside, brush his coat, and make him look presentable again. There are no shortcuts to happiness.

It is convenient to have a selection of grooming tools always at hand, but, in an emergency, your old comb and brush can be very useful. If your dog loses hair so profusely that it makes you wonder if he will have any left tomorrow, daily brushing is the only remedy to his predicament and yours. Dead hair, close to the skin, is the hair he is shedding—the hair you see on your clothes, furniture, and everywhere in the house. Loosened with a brisk massage, it should first be combed then brushed out with a stiff brush.

Whenever you are tired and decide to postpone your dog's grooming, look around you—at your pet and at your home—and remember that things will only be worse tomorrow. It will give you the strength to do it today.

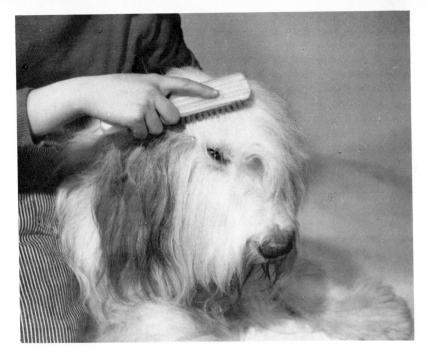

The Old English Sheepdog is all
hair but he hardly sheds. He keeps
his coat year-round, not shedding it
with the seasons. Frequent brushing
with a stiff brush is all he needs
to look well groomed.

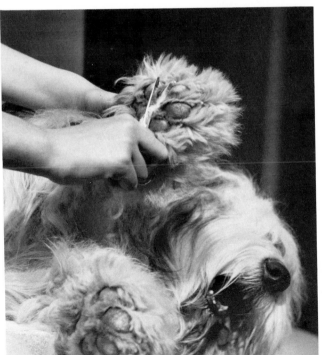

It looks like a painful operation but
it really isn't. The hair between the
dog's toes must be trimmed and
if it's done carefully he should not
feel a thing. Most dogs need such a
trimming about once every six
months. If this hair is allowed to
grow long, it catches all kinds of
dirt, may cause skin troubles
between the toes, and can make
the dog extremely uncomfortable.

91

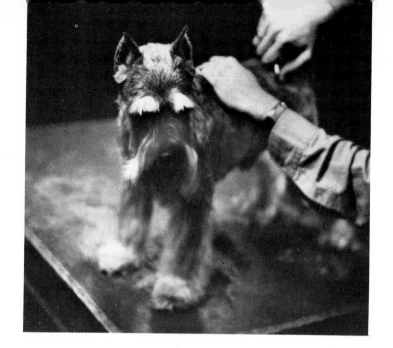

The Miniature Schnauzer is stripped with a stripping knife by a professional groomer. If you like your Schnauzer, don't do it yourself. The tool could become a dangerous weapon in inexperienced hands. Hand stripping takes time and is quite expensive in a grooming parlor. You can have the Schnauzer clipped instead with an electric clipper—it is much quicker and cheaper. The marks left in his coat by the clipper will disappear in a few weeks.

After a conditioning oil lotion is rubbed into the Scottish Terrier's dense coat, a homemade bathrobe is fastened around him. It will keep him warm and prevent the house from getting oily.

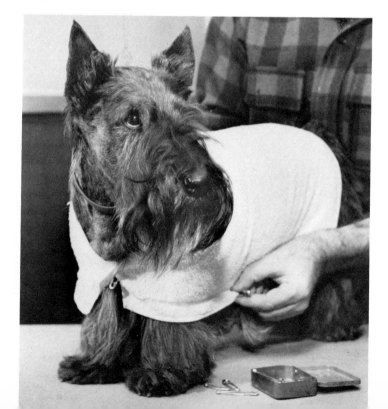

A champion Afghan is groomed every day, but a pet Afghan only needs brushing about once a week. Combing could harm his hair but brushing will make his coat long and silky.

The hair on the Poodle's forehead is brushed, pulled up, and fastened with a ribbon, barrette, or plain rubber band.

The coat is clipped close to the skin but not so close that the skin shows through.

Scissors are used all around for the final touches.

You can groom and clip your poodle yourself if you have time,
patience, books on poodle grooming, and several lessons from a
professional groomer. And, be sure that you can face your poodle
afterwards if you do it wrong. The easier way is to have him groomed
professionally—in between, keeping him in good shape yourself with
a brush and comb.

This Yorkshire knows that to be beautiful one sometimes has to suffer the indignity of walking around rolled up in wrappers. He also must be combed and brushed once a day to keep his silky hair in top condition.

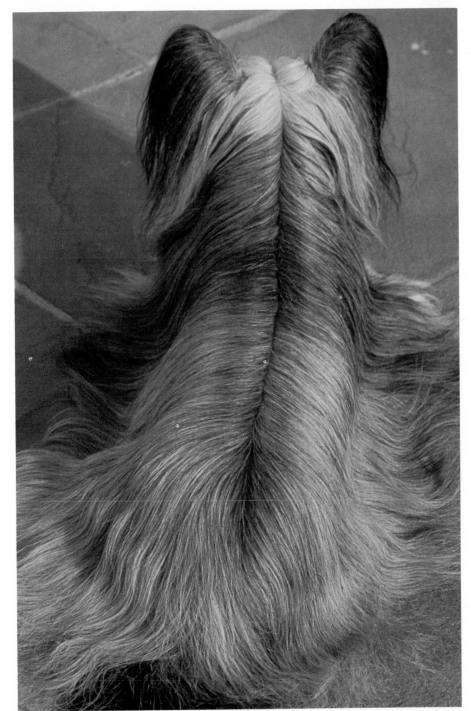

The hair of the Skye Terrier should be parted from head to tail. A brush with long bristles is the only important grooming tool for his coat. Brisk brushing twice a month should make his coat look shiny and well-groomed, with every hair in place.

Long-haired Chihuahuas need an occasional bath. A bathtub is equivalent to a swimming pool for seven of these tiny dogs. Tepid water, mild shampoo, and a smear of oil around their eyelids to prevent soap from getting into their eyes, all make bathing a pleasant event.

In a warm room, bundled up in bath towels,
the Chihuahuas wait to be dried by a
hot-air blower so they will not catch cold.

A Great Dane puppy wears braces on his cropped ears until they can stand up alone.

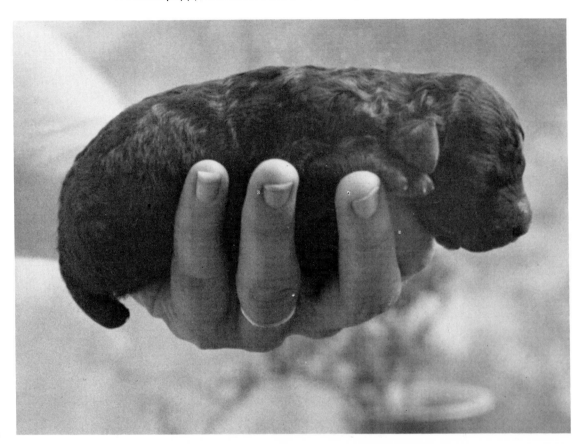

PUPPIES

To me, new-born puppies, like new-born babies, all look alike. But, as time passes, the little flat-faced furpieces will become Yorkshires, Poodles, or Collies. At six weeks or so, when he comes into your home, your puppy will still not look like the breed you expected him to be, but someday he will. You must have faith and be very patient.

It is hard to believe that these puppies will grow up to be elegant, silver-gray, soft-coated, lamb-like Bedlingtons.

The picture of contentment is this mother Bedlington nursing her puppies.

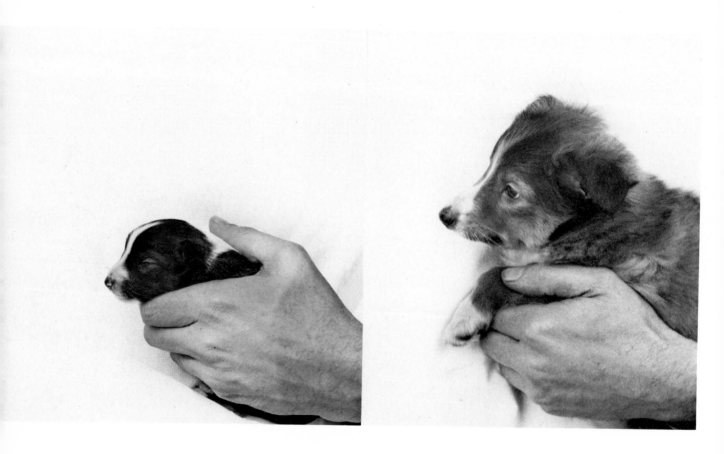

The Shetland Sheepdog is born with the
usual puppy face. But after a few weeks a
Collie profile starts to emerge.

When fully grown, the Sheltie is called the
"Ideal Collie in miniature."

The Australian Terrier puppy has the look of sweet innocence—but only as long as there is not a squirrel or rabbit in sight. Like a true hunter, he runs after them, never successful but always trying.

Two months   Four months   Six months

No Afghan puppy looks like an Afghan. Gradually over the months he transforms from a short-haired, cuddly little dog into a long-legged, big-footed, fluffy adolescent. When two years old, the Afghan is mature and full-grown.

Although puppies are fed several times a day, their appetites are never satisfied. At every feeding time, they seem to be starving.

There is no limit to the capacity of healthy, lively puppies to invent
some mischief—except during the hours they spend sleeping.

Wire-Haired Fox Terrier puppies look like stuffed toys. But, very much alive, they are truly little bundles of energy. When they pause between romps it is only to recharge their batteries for more fun and games.

Three Yorkshire Terriers have plenty of space sharing a corner of a chair. Their ages are one year, three months, and new-born. All Yorkies are born black and weigh a scant two ounces at birth.

Apso Seng Key is the Tibetan name for their watchdog, the Lhasa Apso. Translated it means "the Sentry Dog with the bark of a Lion." This alert Lhasa puppy is ready to live up to his honorable name.